Pre-Adamic Man, Dinosaurs, The Ice Age, And GOD

By: Angela D. Hyman

Acknowledgments

I want to mention three individuals whom God has used as an inspiration to me in writing this book and whose names I've mentioned in the book.

They have been a God-given asset to me for my continued growth in spiritual knowledge and understanding of the surpassing greatness of God the Father, God the Son, God the Holy Spirit, and their Kingdom of Light.

Two have also been extremely instrumental to me in their teaching on The Kingdom of Darkness. As Christians, we are in a spiritual battle with an enemy we need to know in order to defeat him. Sadly, I think that we, as Christians, fall dangerously short of our knowledge and effectiveness in this area.

I thank God for the teachings I've received in this area and more from the following:

Derek Prince Ministries

AND

Benny Hinn Ministries

Lastly, as I refer to science in this book, I want to acknowledge Hugh Ross, a Christian Astrophysicist. Hugh Ross uses his vast knowledge in that field of science to prove the existence of our Triune God! What an amazing testimony! I did not go into the depths of his knowledge in this book, as it did not relate to the title. However, I highly recommend becoming acquainted with his contribution to revealing the greatness of our God in terms of His universe.

Contents

Introduction

"The secret things belong to the Lord our God, but those things which are revealed belong unto us and our children for ever, that we may do all the words of this law." **Deuteronomy 29:29 KJV**

First, I'd like to proclaim that I am a Christian and a follower of Jesus Christ as my Savior and my Lord. However, this book is not about the Gospel message exclusively. Instead, it is about the undetermined period of time and events that occurred after **Genesis 1:1 KJV,** *"In the beginning, God created the heaven(s) and the earth."* And before **Genesis 1:2 KJV,** *"And the earth was without form, and void; and darkness was upon the face of the deep."*

The names given for this period are 'The Gap' or 'The Pre-Adamic Age.' My purpose and intent of this book is to reveal from scriptures found in the Bible that this period did exist. Pre-Adamic man (or races), dinosaurs, and the Ice Age, which occurred during this time, are all spoken about in the Bible.

If you ever had questions regarding these facts, or if you are a skeptic towards the Bible and God, brought on due to the claims of many Christians that the earth is only six thousand years old and that dinosaurs were in Noah's Ark, then I invite you to read this book. This is not a postulated book. This book is an account in which God is speaking by revealing from His word, the Bible, the facts and truths surrounding the title of this book.

However, first I want to make it plain that this book is by no means an attempt to ridicule Christians who choose not to believe the accounts of this book. Also, neither should they ridicule those of us who do believe these accounts as scriptural facts.

It is with great humility that I have accepted from God this assignment as a servant of His will to make known the contents of this book. God's heart is that some who have previously turned away from Him may now open their hearts and want to know Him.

Chapter 1

Science and <u>GOD</u>

"Also He hath set the world (or eternity) in their heart, so that no man can find the work that God worketh from the beginning to the end." **<u>Ecclesiastes 3:11b KJV</u>**

God created everything; therefore, it stands to reason that God created science. Man can use the discipline of science to satisfy the God-given innate desire to know what God reveals of Himself and His creation. However, there are two types of science. One type is 'legitimate' science, which proves the existence of God, and the revelation that God has given of Himself and His creation in the Bible is accurate. The second type of science is 'illegitimate' science which denies the existence of God, such as The Big Bang Theory and The Theory of Evolution, both of which cannot prove the accuracy of the Bible. In fact, the Bible and nature itself are both strong contradictions of illegitimate science.

The only science referred to in this book is 'legitimate' science. I begin this book speaking of science as it relates to God because 'legitimate' science proves that what God has revealed about Himself and His creation in the Bible is accurate. It's not the other way around; the Bible does not prove science. When I first heard Benny Hinn say that, it opened up a well in me that God, through the Bible, continues to fill.

Secondly, science is not a 'bad' or 'evil' word or evil discipline. Especially when it can prove God's existence and His revelations of Himself and His creations are accurate. There is a deep depth of disciplines within science that have proven the accuracy of the Bible and the existence of God. However, this book only scratches the surface of what is relevant to the title, but there is so much more!

I am amazed and overwhelmed with joy when I hear renowned scientists such as astrophysicist Hugh Ross use that knowledge to confirm the existence of our Triune God! I did not even touch upon his work in this book. However, to me, he bears mention. What a testimony!

First of all, it is important to understand that the Bible is a revelation specifically of the Adamic race, all pointing to and leading to The Messiah, Jesus Christ, and The Kingdom of God. The Bible does not deal 'openly' with the races and times before Adam. Although that is not the 'focus' of the Bible, accounts of this period which have been proven by science, are revealed in the Bible. God will reveal the existence of this period, to the point which He has determined, to those who humble themselves and seek Him for this revelation.

The time since the creation of Adam and mankind as we are today is six thousand years. **However, the age of the earth and the universe is approximately fourteen billion years old.** There were also types of 'men' and catastrophic events which took place before the creation of Adam, which are discussed in this book.

Chapter 2
Genesis Chapter 1:1-2

"In the beginning God created the heaven and the earth."
Genesis 1:1 KJV

There are translations from the Hebrew language which are of particular relevance here as follows:

- Beginning = *bereshith* – which means 'dateless past.'
- God = *Elohim* – which is the plural word for God introducing the Trinity of The Father, The Son, and The Holy Spirit.
- Create = *bara* – which means 'brought out of nothing.'
- Heaven = *shamayim* – *heavens* – in Hebrew, the word '*shamayim*' is plural for 'heavens,' **not** 'heaven' as it was translated.

The Bible reveals three heavens as follows:

- 1st – The atmosphere we can see, including the sun, moon, stars, and other planetary bodies.

    Genesis 1:1 KJV *"In the beginning God created the heaven(s) and the earth."*

Genesis 1:16-17 KJV [16] *"And God made two great lights; the greater light to rule the day, and the lesser light to rule the night: he made the stars also. [17] And God set them in the firmament of the heaven to give light upon the earth,"*

- 2nd – The dwelling of the spiritual powers and principalities referred to in **Ephesians 6:12 KJV**, *"For we wrestle not against flesh and blood, but against principalities, against powers, against the rulers of the darkness of this world, against spiritual wickedness in high places."* (high = 'heavenly' places in other translations)

- 3rd – The heaven where God transcends to dwell, as mentioned by the Apostle Paul when he tells of being caught up in the third heaven where he saw God.

  2 Corinthians 12:2 KJV, *"I knew a man in Christ above fourteen years ago, (whether in the body, I cannot tell; or whether out of the body, I cannot tell: God knoweth;) such an one caught up to the third heaven."*

Now let us review **Genesis 1:2.**

Genesis 1:2 KJV, *"And the earth was without form and void, and darkness was upon the face of the deep."*

Again, there are relevant words from the Hebrew language as follows:

- Was = *haya,* which means 'became'
- Without form = *tohu*
- Void = *bohu* – which means 'empty'

<u>When were the angels and heavenly hosts created?</u>

Before we go further, it is necessary to point out that God created the angels and the heavenly hosts **before** He created the earth, as seen in Job:

<u>Job 38:4-7 KJV,</u> *"⁴ Where wast thou when I laid the foundations of the earth? Declare, if thou hast understanding. ⁵ Who hath laid the measures thereof, if thou knowest? Or who hath stretched the line upon it? ⁶ Whereupon are the foundations thereof fastened? Or who laid the corner stone thereof;* **⁷ When the morning stars sang together, And all the sons of God shouted for joy."**

In those verses of Job, God reveals that '**the morning stars sang together (angels) and all the sons of God shouted for joy (also angels) when God laid the foundations of the earth.'** So we see that the angels were present when God created the earth in **<u>Genesis 1:1</u>**, having been created first.

God's character in Genesis 1:1:

Something happened between **Genesis 1:1** and **Genesis 1:2.** God **did not create** "formless" or 'tohu' and "void" or 'empty.' That is not His character nor His way, as the following scriptures will prove.

Here as well as throughout this book, it is important to remember and understand that **the Bible interprets the Bible.**

Deuteronomy 32:4 KJV, *"He is the rock, **His work is perfect:** for all His ways are judgement: A God of truth and without iniquity. Just and right is He."*

Isaiah 45:18 KJV, *"For thus saith the LORD that created the heavens, God Himself formed the earth and made it, he hath established it, **He created it not in vain, He formed it to be inhabited;** I am the LORD, and there is none else."*

Ecclesiastes 3:11a KJV, **"He hath made everything beautiful in its time."**

Psalm: 18:30 KJV, **"As for God, His way is perfect;** *He is a buckler to all those that trust in Him."*

The common theme associated with God's character and His ways that He reveals to us in these scriptures are as follows:

- His **work is perfect.**
- He **created it not in vain,** He **formed it to be inhabited.**
- He hath **made everything beautiful** in his time.
- As **for** God, **His way is perfect.**

<u>What happened to turn **Genesis 1:1** into **Genesis 1:2**?</u>

The question now becomes, what happened to cause the earth to go from its perfect creation state in **<u>Genesis 1:1</u>** to the formless, void, darkened, and flooded state in **<u>Genesis 1:2.</u>** The answer, revealed by God in the Bible, is that it was the result of God's divine judgment, wrath, and abandonment brought about by Lucifer's rebellion.

Lucifer's rebellion was joined by one-third of the angels who were under his charge and sided with him against God. **<u>Revelation 12:4 KJV</u>**, *"And his tail drew the third part of the **stars of heaven,** and did cast them to the earth:"* (**'stars of heaven'** are the angels). The rebellion was also joined by the Pre-Adamic race(s) that God had given Lucifer rulership over whom he provoked against God. (I will cover this further in the next chapter.)

The Bible does not reveal the timespan before, during, or after this event; however, it does reveal its occurrence as proven by the following scriptures.

Jeremiah 4:23–27 KJV:

"23 I beheld the earth, and lo, **it was without form and void, and the heavens and they had no light. 24 I beheld the mountains, and low they trembled and all the hills moved lightly. 25 I beheld and low there was no man, and all the birds of the heaven were fled. 26 I beheld and, lo, the fruitful place was a wilderness and all the cities thereof were broken down at the presence of the LORD, and by His fierce anger.** _27 For thus hath the LORD said, The whole land will be desolate yet will I not make a full end."_

In those verses, we see the revelation the prophet Jeremiah was given by God through a vision of the past. In that vision, Jeremiah was shown God's destruction of the **Genesis 1:1** earth.

From that vision, it is revealed that there was a fruitful place. There were cities, mountains, and hills. He no longer saw man because he had been 'removed' from his cities and fruitful place. He saw birds that fled. Jeremiah was shown the **destruction** of the 'perfect' earth from **Genesis 1:1,** making it into **Genesis 1:2**. (Notice, verse 27 "The whole land will be desolate, **yet I will not make a full end**," as I will refer to it later.)

The Bible bears witness to itself of the above account in several places, including Job's encounter with God, which coincides with Jeremiah's account and also reveals additional information.

Job 9:4-7 KJV:

*"⁴ He is wise in heart and mighty in strength: who hath hardened himself against Him and hath prospered? ⁵ Which **removeth the mountains,** and they know not: Which **overturneth them in His anger**. ⁶ Which shaketh the earth out of her place, and the pillars thereof tremble. ³ **Which commandeth the sun and it riseth not, and sealest up the stars.** ⁸ Which alone spreadeth out the heavens and treadth upon the waves of the sea.* (Verse 8 describes what begins in Genesis 1:3).

The above verses from Job give witness to Jeremiah's vision. Both speak of God removing and overturning mountains in His anger. Job's account also reveals additional important information as follows, **which commandeth the sun and it riseth not, and sealest up the stars.** Remember... *'darkness over the face of the deep' from* **Genesis 1:2.**

Another witness from the Bible giving revelation of this account is found in the prophet Isaiah–which also includes additional revelation.

Isaiah 24:1 KJV:

*"Behold the LORD maketh the earth empty, and maketh it waste **and turneth it upside down, and scattereth abroad its inhabitants.**"*

That verse is amazing! **'and turneth it upside down,'**! Total destruction, which clearly has **not** happened since the creation of Adam. If it did, then none of us would be here today!

There is also another witness from Job revealing relevant information from God's discourse with Job.

Job 25:28–30 KJV:

*"²⁸ Hath the rain a father? Or who hath begotten the drops of dew? ²⁹ Out of whose womb came the ice? And the hoary frost of heaven, who hath gendered it? ³⁰ **The waters are hid with a stone, and the face of the deep is frozen.**"*

'The waters are hid with a stone and the face of the deep is frozen.' This reveals the Ice Age of sudden and total destruction. I will discuss this further in Chapter 5.

Now you may say that all of these revelations are from the Old Testament. Is there a witness in the New Testament? The answer is yes, in 2 Peter.

2 Peter 3:3-7 KJV:

*"³Knowing this first, that there shall come in the last days scoffers, walking after their own lusts, ⁴ and saying, Where is the promise of His coming? for since the fathers fell asleep, all things continue as they were from the beginning of creation. ⁵ For this they willingly are ignorant of, that by the word of God the heavens were of old, **and the earth standing out of the water and in the water ⁶ whereby the earth that then was, being overflowed with water perished, ⁷** but the heavens and the earth, which are now, by the same word are kept in store, reserved unto fire against the day of judgement and perdition of ungodly men."*

Peter is speaking of the revelation he received by the Holy Spirit of the destruction of the earth "standing out of water and in water," which took place between **Genesis 1:1** and **Genesis 1:2**, in which the 'earth perished.'

He is not referring to the flood of Noah's time because in that flood, eight people, plus two of each animal type, were saved, and the **earth was not destroyed.**

Chapter Conclusion:

None of these verses are prophetic toward the future. They are not referring to the second coming of Jesus and the millennial reign. Instead, they are all revelations given by God of a time span after **Genesis 1:1 KJV,** *"In the beginning God created the heaven(s) and the earth,"* which resulted in **Genesis 1:2 KJV,** *"And the earth was without form, and void; and darkness was upon the face of the deep."*

God did not **create** formless, dark, empty, void, and flooded; instead, He **caused** it. Let us 'see' what He reveals to us about that time that provoked Him to destroy His perfect creation of the earth in the next chapter.

Chapter 3

Lucifer's Reign of the Pre-Adamic Race(s)

I've entitled this chapter 'Lucifer's Reign' because he did have a God-given reign over the Pre-Adamic race(s) and one-third of the angels (as an Archangel, he had that authority over one-third of the angels). It is important to know and understand this fact as it is revealed to us by scriptures in the Bible. This also enables us to have a better understanding of the time before Adam.

Many people, including Christians, ask why did God create Satan? The answer to that question is God did **not** create Satan. God created Lucifer. Lucifer, all the angels, and the Pre-Adamic race(s) were **all** created with free will, just like we are.

<u>Who was Lucifer?</u>

The Bible introduces us to Lucifer in the book of Isaiah. Let's have a look.

<u>**Isaiah:14:12–15 KJV:**</u>

*"12 How art thou fallen from heaven, O Lucifer, son of the morning! how art thou cut down to the ground, **which didst weaken the nations.** 13 For thou hast said in thine heart, **I will ascend into heaven, I will exalt my throne** above the stars of God; I will sit also on the mount of the congregation, in the sides of the north. 14 **I will ascend above the heights of the clouds; I** will be like the most High. 15 **Yet thou shalt be brought down to hell, to the sides of the pit.**"*

The portions of the verses I've highlighted substantiate the fact that God had given Lucifer rule over the earth and its Pre-Adamic inhabitants at that time as follows:

- *Weaken* the nations – Nations existed **before** Adam.
- I will **ascend into heaven** – He was on the earth.
- I will **exalt my throne** – He had a **throne** since he was a ruler.
- Satan was ***brought down to hell, to the sides of the pit.*** Satan was cast out of heaven (where he led his rebellion) to the **pit,** which is hell; however, he was not bound there. He was able to revisit the restored earth.

There is an additional revelation of Lucifer given to the prophet Ezekiel.

Ezekiel 28:11-19 KJV:

"¹¹ Moreover the word of the LORD came to me. ¹² Son of man, take up a lamentation upon the King of Tyrus and say to him, Thus saith the LORD God; Thou sealest up the sum, full of wisdom and perfect in beauty. ¹³ **Thou hast been in Eden the garden of God,** *every precious stone was thy covering, the sardius, topaz, and diamond, the beryl, the onyx, and the jasper, the sapphire, the emerald and the carbuncle, and gold; the workmanship of thy tabrets and of thy pipes was prepared in the in the day that thou wast created. ¹⁴ Thou art the anointed cherub that covereth, and I have set thee so; thou wast upon the holy mountain of God; thou hast walked up and down in the midst of the stones of fire. ¹⁵ Thou was perfect in thy ways from the day thou wast created, till iniquity was found in thee.¹⁶ By the multitude of thy merchandise they have filled the midst of thee with violence, and now thou hast sinned:* **Therefore I will cast thee out as a profane out of the mountain of God;** *and I will destroy thee, O covering cherub from the midst of the stones of fire. ¹⁷Thine heart was lifted up because of thy beauty, thou hast corrupted thy wisdom by reason of brightness; I will cast*

thee to the ground, I will lay thee before kings, that they may behold thee. ^{18} **Thou hast defiled thy sanctuaries** *by the multitude of thy iniquity of thy traffic; therefore will I bring forth a fire from the midst of thee, it shall devour thee, and it shall bring thee to ashes on the earth in the sight of all them that behold thee. ^{19}All they that know thee among the people shall be astonished at thee;* **thou shall be a terror and never shall thou be anymore."**

The portions of the verses highlighted give additional revelation on Lucifer's God-given rule on earth with the Pre-Adamic race(s) as follows:

- Thou hast **been in Eden, the garden of God**. Notice Lucifer was there in all his splendor. This was the **Pre-Adamic Garden of Eden.**
- Cast out of the '**mountain of God,**' which is God's government or God's Kingdom.
- Thou hast **defiled thy sanctuaries** – He was the leader of worship to God on the earth at that time, which he defiled.
- Notice that verse **19b** is also a prophetic verse referring to Satan's final demise revealed in the book of **Revelation 12:7-10 KJV,** *"And there was war in heaven: Michael and his angels fought against the dragon; and the dragon fought and his angels, ^{8} and prevailed not, neither was their place found any more in heaven. ^{9} And the great dragon*

was cast out, that old serpent, called the Devil, and Satan, which deceiveth the whole world: he was cast out into the earth, and his angels were cast out with him. [10] And I heard a loud voice saying in heaven, **Now is come salvation, and strength, and the kingdom of our God, and the power of his Christ: for the accuser of our brethren is cast down, which accused them before our God day and night."**

(Notice that those verses are **not** referring to the Pre-Adamic war incited by Satan in heaven. The highlighted portion is confirmation of that).

Before I conclude this chapter, I think it necessary to discuss the **realities of Hell.** Heaven is real, and so is Hell. Hell was not created for man. There was no Adamic race when Hell was created. Hell was created for Satan, the fallen angels, and the Pre-Adamic race(s) who joined Satan's rebellion. Hell is now a place of 'eternal torment' for those who **choose** not to believe in The Gospel of Jesus Christ.

Chapter Conclusion:

From the revelations given to us by God in the above verses of **Isaiah** and **Ezekiel**, we see that God gave Lucifer rule over the earth. Earth was inhabited by a

Pre-Adamic race(s) under Lucifer's reign. There was a Pre-Adamic Garden of Eden that Lucifer ruled while adorned in all of his splendor. This Pre-Adamic Garden of Eden included a temple and a sacred mountain. Lucifer was the guardian of the temple and directed the worship of God.

Lucifer defiled that worship and turned the inhabitants and one-third of the angels under his rule against God. God responded with divine judgment, wrath, and abandonment of the earth in **Genesis 1:1,** resulting in the earth of **Genesis 1:2**.

As I mentioned previously, the time period of Lucifer's reign and his rebellion are not revealed in the Bible. However, the age of the earth and the universe suggest billions of years!

Now Lucifer has become Satan:

It is very clear from scripture that Lucifer, who became Satan, the adversary of God and man, the slanderer and accuser, entered the ***Adamic Garden of Eden*** on the *'restored'* earth as the 'serpent' who usurped Adam's God-given authority.

In doing so, he regained his authority over the earth with his 'kingdom of darkness.' God told Adam to 'subdue' the earth and have dominion over all the animals. **Genesis 1:28 KJV,** *"And God blessed them,* *and God said unto them, Be fruitful, and multiply, and replenish the earth, **and subdue it**: and have dominion over the fish of the sea, and over the fowl of the air, and over every living thing that moveth upon the earth."* He was supposed to 'subdue' Satan, and, as we know, Adam failed.

<u>What happened to the Pre-Adamic race (s) destroyed by God?</u>

The Pre-Adamic race(s) judged by God at that time for their rebellion against Him, led by then Lucifer, now occupy the 'Pit.' They also roam the earth as 'persons without bodies' who are the 'demons' we encounter and fight spiritual battles with today. Satan is still their leader, as head of the kingdom of darkness.

Let us look at a revelation of this in the New Testament with the encounter of Jesus with the man possessed by the Legion of demons. **Mark 5: 1–10 KJV,** *"¹ And they came over unto the other side of the sea, into the country of the Gadarenes. ² And when he was come out of the ship, immediately there met him out of the tombs a man with an unclean spirit, ³ who had his dwelling among the tombs, and no man could bind him, no, not with chains: ⁴ because that he had been often bound with fetters and chains, and the chains had been plucked asunder by him, and the fetters broken in pieces: neither* *could any man tame him. [5] And always, night and day, he was in the mountains, and in the tombs, crying and cutting himself with stones. [6] But when he saw Jesus afar off, he ran and worshipped him, [7] and cried in a loud voice, and said, What have I to do with thee, Jesus, thou Son of the most high God? I adjure thee by God, that thou torment me not. [8] For He said unto him, 'come out of the man thou unclean spirit.' [9] And He asked him, What is thy name? And he answered, saying, My name is Legion for we are many. [10]* **And he besought him much that He would not send them out of the country."**

Or as stated in **Luke 8:31 KJV, "And they besought Him that He would not command them to go out into the deep."**

Luke 8:31 NIV, "And they begged Jesus repeatedly not to order them to go to the Abyss."

We can see from this account how the demons begged Jesus not to send them out of the country, or into the deep, or to the Abyss. That is where they were sent by God, along with one-third of the angels, who joined Lucifer's rebellion against God. Lucifer was also sent there, as revealed in **Isaiah 12:15 KJV,** *"[15]Yet thou shalt be brought down to hell, to the sides of the pit."*

Jesus also reveals this fact; **Luke 10:18 KJV** *"And he said unto them, I beheld Satan as lightning fall from heaven."*

How is Satan now in the **second heaven**?

There, in the pit and the abandoned earth, Satan waited until God **restored** the earth and created Adam (a name for both male and female). Then Satan saw an opportune time to destroy the fellowship God had and loved with His creation, made in His own image. Satan devised a scheme to steal from Adam his God-given dominion over the earth.

Once Satan reclaimed the rule and occupation of the earth due to the sin of Adam, he also reclaimed habitation in the second heaven. Satan also released some demons from the pit to do his bidding in his kingdom of darkness. It's revealed in the Book of Revelation that there is coming a time when the demons still in the pit will be released to torment the inhabitants of the earth who curse God and worship the Anti-Christ. **Revelation 9:2–11 KJV,** *"² And he opened the bottomless pit, and there arose a smoke of a great furnace; and the sun and the air were darkened by reason of the smoke of the pit. ³ And there came out of the smoke locusts upon the earth and unto them was given power, as the scorpions of the earth have power. ⁴ And it was commanded them that they should not hurt the grass* *of the earth, neither any green thing, neither any tree, but only those men which have not the seal of God in their foreheads. ⁵ And to them it was given that they should not kill them, but that they should be tormented five months."*

<u>Are demons fallen or inerrant angels?</u>

There are some in the body of Christ who believe that demons are the fallen or inerrant angels. However, I believe that the Bible is clear that angels (referring now to the non-rebellious only) are heaven bound with spiritual bodies. Angels have fully manifested in human appearance many times in the Bible. Also, we are exhorted by the writer of Hebrews: **Hebrews 13:2 <u>KJV</u>,** *"Be not forgetful to entertain strangers: for thereby some have entertained angels unaware."*

Demons, on the other hand, are earth and hell bound and are 'persons without bodies' seeking a body to occupy. That is a perfect description of demons by the late Derek Prince. The habitation of the fallen or inerrant angels in their spiritual bodies is described in the next two paragraphs.

<u>Habitation of 'fallen' or 'inerrant' angels</u>

Once Satan reclaimed a place and reign on earth, due to Adam's rebellion, now Satan and some of the fallen angels occupy the second heaven as the 'powers and principalities' referred to in **Ephesians 6:12 KJV,** *"12For we wrestle not against flesh and blood, but against principalities, against powers, against the rulers of the darkness of this world, against spiritual wickedness in high (other translations say 'heavenly') places."*

This warfare activity in the <u>heavenlies</u> is revealed in the book of **Daniel 10:12-13 KJV,** *"12 Then he said unto me, Fear not, Daniel: for from the first day that thou didst set thine heart to understand, and to chasten thyself before thy God, thy words <u>were</u> heard, and I come for thy words. 13 But the prince of the kingdom of Persia withstood me one and twenty days: but lo, Michael, one of the chief princes, came to help me, and I remained there with the kings of Persia."*

<u>Rebellious angels who are bound in hell:</u>

There were also rebellious angels who are now in hell chained in darkness, as seen in **2 Peter 2:4a KJV,** *"For if God spared not the angels that sinned, but cast them down to hell, and delivered them into chains of darkness, to be reserved unto judgement."*

This is also revealed in **Jude 1:6 KJV,** *"And angels which kept not their first estate, but left their own habitation, he hath reserved in everlasting chains under* *darkness unto the judgement of the great day.*" These were the angels who slept with women and had children with them who became giants called 'the Nephilim.'

The above-mentioned account is revealed in **Genesis 6:1-2 & 4 KJV,** *"¹And it came to pass when men began to multiply on the face of the earth, and daughters were born unto them,² that the **sons of God** saw the daughters of men that they were fair, and they took them wives of all which they chose. ⁴There were giants in the earth in those days; and also after that, when the sons of God came unto the daughters of men, and they bare children to them,"*

That was Satan's plan to contaminate the 'seed of the woman' who would bear The Messiah revealed in **Genesis 3:15 KJV,** *"¹⁵ and I will put enmity between thee and the woman, and between thy seed and her seed; it shall bruise thy head, and thou shall bruise his heel."*

God destroyed this contaminated seed in the flood of Noah, revealed in **Genesis 6:15-18 KJV,** ***"¹⁵ And GOD saw that the wickedness of man was great in the earth, and that every imagination of the thoughts of his heart was only evil continually.*** *¹⁶ And it repented the LORD that he had made man on the earth, and it grieved him at his heart.*

¹⁷ And the LORD said, I will destroy man whom I have created from the face of the earth, both man, and beast, and the creeping thing, and the fowls of the air, for it repenteth me that I have made them. ¹⁸ But Noah found grace in the eyes of the LORD."

"¹⁵ And GOD saw that the wickedness of man was great in the earth, and that every imagination of the thoughts of his heart was only evil continually." This verse reveals the condition of man's heart during that time, which grieved God to the point of destroying him. So, we see that it wasn't the result of Satan's scheme to contaminate the seed of the woman alone, which caused God to destroy the earth's inhabitants at that time. How many choose to be a 'Noah' in today's world?

I want to also point out that God's destruction of Satan's first plan to block the Messiah did not stop him from trying again. In the books of **Kings** and **Chronicles**, there are accounts of Satan's attempts to destroy the lineage to the Messiah, **but GOD ...!**

I have elaborated on the facts given from scripture in the above paragraphs as an aide to give understanding to the time and events which occurred between **Genesis 1:1** and **Genesis 1:2.** All that I have referenced are revelations given by God in the Bible and **not** my own imagination.

Chapter 4

Dinosaurs Revealed in the Book of Job

Now, let's look at dinosaurs. Science has discovered the existence of dinosaurs, and we can see their bones fully assembled in museums. These dinosaurs were **not** on Noah's Ark! These dinosaurs are **65 million years old,** not six thousand years young! The dinosaurs existed during the time between **Genesis 1:1** and **Genesis 1:2**. As I stated previously, 'legitimate' science proves the accuracy of the Bible, and it is **not** the other way around.

Dinosaurs are mentioned in the Bible in the book of Job during God's discourse with Job.

However, we must understand that dinosaurs are mentioned alongside animals that exist today. This is a format of 'dual description,' which is used in many places in the Bible. In the book of Job, chapters 40 and 41, this format is used to describe the difference between Pre-Adamic and Adamic animals.

The most infamous portion of scripture which was inspired by 'dual description' is **Ezekiel 28:1-19.** In that chapter, we have a 'prince' of Tyrus who was a man, and a king of Tyrus who was Lucifer and today is Satan.

God did not give a description of every dinosaur or every animal in His discourse with Job. However, what He did give us is in line with other scripture, legitimate science, and nature.

Please join me now in an 'excavation' of the animals and their types in Job chapters 40 and 41:

Job 40:15-24 KJV:

"^{*15*} *Behold now* **behemoth, Which I made along with thee;** *he eateth grass as an ox.* ^{*16*} *Lo now, his strength is in his loins, And his force is in the navel of his belly.*

- Here the Lord is describing the **hippopotamus. 'Which I made along with thee'** statement, including the description, is a clear indication of the hippopotamus. The **hippopotamus was in Noah's Ark.**

Job 40:17-19 KJV:

"^{*17*}*He moveth his* **tail like a cedar;** *the sinews of his stones are wrapped together.* ^{*18*} *His bones are as strong pieces of brass, His bones are like bars of iron.* ^{*19*} *He is*

chief of the ways of God: He that maketh him can make his sword to approach unto him."

- This description is **not** of the hippopotamus; it is of a **dinosaur** with a **'tail like a cedar,'** and the other characteristics mentioned make it clear. **This dinosaur became extinct 65 million years ago and was not in Noah's Ark.**

Job 40:20–24 KJV:

"20 Surely the mountains bring him forth food, Where all the beasts of the field play. 21 He lieth under the shady trees in the covert of the reed, and fens. 22 The shady trees cover him with their shadow; The willows of the brook compass him about. 23 Behold, he drinketh up a river and hasteth not; He trusteth that he can draw up the Jordan into his mouth. 24 He taketh it with his eyes; His nose can pierceth through snares."

- This description is again of the **hippopotamus.** (Back and forth of the 'dual description' format).

Job 41:1–34 KJV:

*"1 Canst thou draw out **leviathan** with a hook? or his tongue with a cord which thou lettest down? 2 Canst*

thou put an hook into his nose? *³Will he make many supplications unto thee? Will he speak soft words unto thee?* *⁴ Will he make a covenant with thee? Will thou take him for a servant for ever?* *⁵ Will thou play with him as with a bird? Or will thou bind for thy maidens?* *⁴ Shall the companions make a banquet of him? Shall they part him among the merchants?* *⁷ Canst thou fill his skin with barbed irons? Or his head with fish spears?* *⁸ Lay thine hand upon him, Remember the battle, do no more.*"

- This portion of the 'leviathan' description belongs to a **crocodile,** as all the questions and comments reveal. **The crocodile was aboard Noah's Ark.**

<u>Job 41:9–12 KJV:</u>

"Behold, the hope of him is in vain: Shall not one be cast down even at the sight of him? *¹⁰ None is so fierce that dare stir him up: Who then is able to stand before me?* *¹¹ Who hath prevented me, that I should repay him? Whatsoever is under the whole heaven is mine.* *¹² I will not conceal his parts, Nor his power, nor his comely proportion.*"

- Here the Lord gives a 'peek' of the **leviathan as a dinosaur**, which He will add more detail to in verses to follow.

Job 41:13-17 KJV:

"13 Who can discover the face of his garment? Or who can come to him with his double bridle? 14 Who can open the doors of his face? His teeth are terrible round about. 15 His scales are his pride, shut up together as with a close seal. 16 One is so near to another, That no air can come between them. 17 they are joined to one another, They stick together, that they cannot be sundered."

- This is, again, a description of the **leviathan as the crocodile**. (Again, we see the back and forth of 'dual description')

Job 41:18-34 KJV:

"By his neesings a light doth shine, And his eyes are like the eyelids of the morning. 19 Out of his mouth go burning lamps, And sparks of fire leap out. 20 Out of his nostrils goeth smoke as out of a seething pot or caldron. 21 His breath kindleth coals, And a flame goeth out of his mouth. 22 In his neck remaineth strength, And sorrow is turned to joy before him. 23 The flakes of his flesh are joined together: They are firm in themselves; they cannot be removed. 24 His heart is as firm as a stone; Yea, as hard as a piece of nether millstone. 25 When he raiseth up himself, the mighty are afraid: By reason of breakings

they purify themselves. *26 The sword of him that layeth at him cannot hold: The spear, the dart, nor the habergeon. 27He esteemeth iron as straw, And brass as rotten wood. 28 The arrow cannot make him flee: Slingstones are turned with him into stubble. 29 Darts are counted as stubble: He laugheth at the shaking spear. 30Sharp stones are under him. He spreadth sharp pointed things upon the mire. 31 He maketh the deep to boil like a pot: he maketh the sea like a pot of ointment. 32 He maketh a path to shine after him; One would think the deep to be hoary. 33Upon earth there is not his like, Who is made without fear. 34 He beholdeth all high things: He is a king over all the children of pride."*

- Verses 18 – 34 again describe the **leviathan as a dinosaur,** as well as what could be a **dragon!** Again, **this dinosaur and/or dragon was not in Noah's Ark, as it became extinct 65 million years ago.**

Chapter Conclusion:

It is clear to see from the above verses in Job chapters 40–41 that God has revealed to us His creation of dinosaurs. He did this in a 'dual description' format alongside other animals that are **not** dinosaurs, and that exist today.

God has also revealed that the Pre-Adamic race(s) existed **with** the dinosaurs. We can see that from His descriptions of Pre -Adamic man's co-habitation with the dinosaurs.

Now we know from 'legitimate' science that dinosaurs became extinct 65 million years ago. This is one 'pinpoint' of the time frame between <u>Genesis 1:1</u> and <u>Genesis 1:2</u> that God has revealed to us. There is much more that 'legitimate' science and nature has unmasked. However, I'm only touching on a very small amount of what is relevant to the book's title.

Chapter 5

The Ice Age Extinction of Dinosaurs

Although there are several scientific theories on the causes of the events leading up to the destruction and extinction of the dinosaurs, in this book, I will only address the event that has been repeatedly proven by science, which is the **'ice age extinction.'**

What is an 'ice age'?

"An **ice age** is a long period of reduction in the temperature of the earth's surface and atmosphere, resulting in the presence or expansion of continental and polar ice sheets and alpine glaciers." – Wikipedia

"An ice age is a period of colder global temperatures and recurring glacial expansion capable of lasting hundreds of millions of years." – www.history.com

According to science, there have been five major ice ages in earth's history, dating as far back as 2 billion years. However, for the purpose of this book, I am referring only to the fifth ice age, which scientists say wiped out the dinosaurs 65 million years ago.

<u>What science has to say about Ice Age Extinctions:</u>

An article from 'The Museum of Art & Science' MOAS, written by 'James "Zach" Zacharias,' the Senior Curator of Education and History (written in 2020), has some interesting details.

'Ice Age Extinctions — what happened?'

Scientists 3 criteria for extinction events:

1. *The event must be worldwide - animals must be affected over the entire globe.*
2. The extinction event **must happen very quickly** on a short geologic scale.
3. One-third of all existing species must disappear.

According to a scientific theory, there have been five major extinction events called the 'Big Five.' According to this theory, the 5th and most famous event is the catastrophe that wiped out the dinosaurs, which is called the End-Cretaceous event. (I've included the name 'End-Cretaceous' as a reference only).

'What scientists have theorized as **'the smoking gun'** — **a large asteroid** that hit the earth 65 million years ago creating a global meltdown of plant life and ecosystems which ended the 250-million-year reign of the dinosaurs.'

What does the Bible have to say?

The Bible **bears** witness to this 'smoking gun' found in the book of Job as follows:

Job 38:28–30 KJV:

"28 Hath the rain a father? Or who has begotten the drops of dew? 29 Out of whose womb came the ice? And the hoary frost of heaven, who hath gendered it? 30 **The waters are hid with a stone, and the face of the deep is frozen."**

This is God speaking in His discourse with Job. Here God is asking Job who made the rain, the dew, or the ice. Then God tells Job in verse *"30* **The waters are hid with a stone, and the face of the deep is frozen."**

Here God is revealing what science calls an '**asteroid**' as '**a stone**.' When this verse was written in the Hebrew language and translated into the English language, neither had the word 'asteroid.' However, the 'asteroid' is clearly revealed in this verse, and its impact on the earth **was not by accident or 'chance.'**

This is also in line with the scientific criteria of an extinction event.

The event must be worldwide – animals must be affected over the entire globe. The extinction event **must happen very quickly**.

Scientists have discovered that the extinction of the dinosaurs was **sudden**! Scientists have also found pre-historic animals frozen in the ice with food still in their mouths!

<u>Where did all this ice come from, and what happened to the sun?</u>

There are also theories that speculate that ash and soot from massive volcanic activity covered the sun, prohibiting its light and causing the earth to 'darken.' According to this theory, the absence of the sun destroyed the atmosphere and caused the ice age that wiped out the dinosaurs.

The Bible bears witness to what **actually** happened to the sun in the book of Job as follows.

Job 9:4-7 KJV:

"4 He is wise in heart and mighty in strength: who hath hardened himself against Him and hath prospered? 5 Which

removeth the mountains, and they know not: which overturneth them in His anger. ⁶ Which shaketh the earth out of her place, and the pillars thereof tremble. ⁹ **Which commandeth the sun and it riseth not, and sealest up the stars."**

There is so much in these verses! Verses 5 and 6 bear witness to the scientific theories of massive volcanic activity and destruction causing the shifting of the continents!

However, here I just want to focus on **why** the sun was hidden, and that is because **God commanded the sun not to shine!** He also sealed up the stars!

Chapter Conclusion:

From the above scriptures, we can clearly see what God chose to reveal to us about that time period. We see that God himself was the 'catalyst' of the ice age that suddenly destroyed the dinosaurs and the Pre-Adamic race(s) existing with them at that time.

We can also see again how 'legitimate' science proves the accuracy of the Bible.

Dinosaurs were **not** created in <u>**Genesis 1:24-25.**</u> They were created and existed billions of years before then and were destroyed by God when He destroyed the earth of **<u>Genesis 1:1</u>**. Thereby, dinosaurs became extinct 65 million years ago!

During the 14 billion years of existence of the earth and the universe, there have been many discoveries by science of activities, some of which were devastating, occurring during that vast amount of time. They are all known as 'theories,' and I'll mention again that some are 'legitimate,' proving the accuracy of the Bible and the existence of God, while some are not. I have only barely scratched the surface of what is available with what I have presented in reference to the title of this book.

Chapter 6

Genesis Chapter 1:2b-25 & 3:1-3

GOD'S Restoration of Earth and Creation of Animals and Man

Before I begin with 'God's **Restoration** of Earth' through the verses of **Genesis 1:2b-25 & 3:1-3**, it is necessary to give meanings of the following words from the Hebrew language as follows:

- The word **'let'** in Hebrew is a verb that means enable, make possible, grant, allow, permit, and sanction.
- The word **'made'** or **'make'** in Hebrew is an adjective that means done, performed, manufactured, or prepared.
- The word **'create'** in Hebrew means 'out of nothing.'

Now, let's look at the difference between the definitions of the words **'made'** and **'create'** in English from www. learningenglish.voanews.com.

<u>What is the difference between 'made' and 'create'?</u>

- The use of the verb **'make' (or made)** tells us that the production processes and the vehicle (or clothing designs) already existed.
- The verb **'create'** usually suggests newness or innovation. Generally, it means to produce something new or bring something into existence.

The above definitions are derived from the English language. Now, let's look at the same words from Hebrew as follows.

- The Hebrew word for **'create,'** which is **'bara,'** means bringing something into existence out of nothing by the power of God. As seen in **<u>Genesis 1:1 KJV</u>**, *"In the beginning God created the heaven(s) and the earth."*
- The Hebrew word for **'make'** or **'made'** is **'asah,'** which means bringing something into existence by working with or using things <u>that were previously created.</u>

It is very significant that we grasp the difference in the meaning of these words to understand the 'fullness' of the revelation God has given us in **<u>Genesis 1:2b–25 &</u>**

<u>**3:1-3.**</u> As I proceed to exegete these scriptures, I'll be referring to the above definitions.

[*Exegete definition:* The process of discovering the original and intended meaning of a passage of scripture.]

I'll begin with Genesis 1:2 and walk us through God's **'restoration'** and **'creation.'**

<u>**Genesis 1:2 KJV**</u>, *"And the earth was without form, and void; and darkness was upon the face of the deep! <u>And the Spirit of God moved upon the face of the waters.</u>"*

Here we see the Holy Spirit moving upon the face of the waters of the once-perfect earth, which He had previously destroyed. However, God had given His intentions of **'restoration'** by the prophet Jeremiah.

<u>**Jeremiah 4:27,**</u> *"For thus the LORD said; The whole land will be desolate,* **yet I will not make a full end."**

<u>The beginning of God's 'restoration':</u>

Now, keeping Jeremiah 4:27 in mind, let's walk through God's **process** of **restoration.**

<u>**Genesis 1:3-5 KJV**</u>, *"³ And God said, **'let'** <u>there be light and there was light.</u> ⁴ And God saw the light that it was good: And God divided the light from the darkness.*

⁵ And God called the light Day, and the darkness He called Night. And the evening and the morning were the first day."

Here we see the first usage of the Hebrew word for **'let,'** which as seen from the definitions above, refers to **'permission'** and **not** creation.

*"And God said, **'let'** there be light and there was light."* Here God is giving the sun, which He had commanded not to shine in **Job 9:7a KJV**, ***"Which commandeth the sun and it riseth not,"*** the 'permission' to give forth light, although He had not yet restored its position. He divided that light from the darkness and named it Day. The darkness He allowed to remain, He named Night. This is the first act of restoration, showing that the source of the light **already** existed.

I want to point out that it is not clear from scripture the origin of the flood waters covering the earth at that time. We don't know if it was from God's presence, or the light He called forth, melting an ice age, or if it was from a period when it rained on the earth for 2 million years straight. The things that God does not reveal are His *'secrets'* (**Deuteronomy 29:29**), and we should respect that. What He has revealed is that the earth was flooded.

God's restoration 'continues':

Genesis 1:6–9 KJV, *⁶ "And God said, **Let** there be a firmament in the mist of the waters from the waters. ⁷ And God made the firmament and divided the waters which were under the firmament from the waters which were above the firmament: and it was so. ⁸ And God called the firmament Heaven. ⁹ And the evening and the morning were the second day."*

Here on the second day, God separates the waters from the firmament restoring the heavens.

God's restoration 'continues':

Genesis 1:9–13 KJV, *"⁹ And God said, **Let** the waters under the heaven be gathered together unto one place, and **let** the dry land appear and it was so. ¹⁰ And God called the dry land Earth and the gathering together of the waters called He Seas: And God saw that it was good. ¹¹ And God said, **Let** the earth bring forth grass, the herb yielding seed, and the fruit tree yielding fruit after his kind, whose seed is in itself upon the earth: and it was so. ¹² And the earth brought forth grass and herb yielding seed after his kind, and tree yielding fruit whose seed was in itself after his kind and God saw that it was good. ¹³ And the evening and the morning were the third day."*

Here on the third day, we see God again saying '**let,**' thereby giving **permission** and instruction for the separation of the water and the land—calling the dry land Earth and the gathered waters Seas.

God also gives **permission** for the **restoration** of the grass, herbs, and fruit bearing trees which He had originally created in **Genesis 1:1**. Recall again that God did not bring the earth to a full end as revealed in **Jeremiah 4:27**. He now calls forth the restoration of what He had previously created in Genesis 1:1.

God's restoration 'continues':

Genesis 1:14–19 KJV, *[14] "And God said, **Let** there be lights in the firmament of heaven to divide the day from the night, and let them be for signs, and for seasons, and for days, and years: [15] and let them be for lights in the firmament of the heaven to give light upon the earth: and it was so. [16] And God **made** two great lights, the greater light to rule the day and the lesser light to rule the night: He made the stars also. [17] And God set them in the firmament of the heaven to give light upon the earth, [18] and to rule over the day and over the night, and to divide the light from the darkness: and God saw that it was good. [19] And the evening and the morning were the fourth day."*

On the fourth day, God gives permission to **restore** the atmosphere. He 'calls' back the stars, the sun, and the moon to their orbital position. He **made** them and set them in place by calling them back. They were already created in **Genesis 1:1.**

<u>**Now** God begins 'creating'</u>:

Genesis 1:20-23 KJV, *"20And God said Let the waters bring forth abundantly the moving creature that hath life, and fowl that may fly above the earth in the open firmament of heaven. 21And God **created** great whales, and every living creature that moveth, which the waters brought forth abundantly after their kind, and every winged fowl after his kind: and God saw that it was good. 22 And God blessed them, saying, Be fruitful, and multiply, and fill the waters in the seas, and let the fowl multiply in the earth. 23 And the evening and the morning were the fifth day."*

Here on the fifth day, the word **create** is first used. God **creates new creatures** by **speaking** them into existence. He gives the seas and the firmament of heaven permission to receive them. He did **not** restore creatures that he had previously destroyed.

<u>God continues to 'create'</u>:

Genesis 1:24-25 KJV, *24 "And God said, **Let** the earth bring forth the living creature after his kind, cattle,*

and creeping thing, and beast of the earth after his kind: and it was so. ²⁵ *And God **'made'** the beast of the earth after his kind, and the cattle after their kind, and every thing that creepeth upon the earth after his kind: and God saw that it was good.*

Here God continues His creation by **'making'** the land animals. In **'making'** them, God used the dust of the ground, which He had previously **created** in **Genesis 1:1.** We see this depicted in **Genesis 2:19a,** *"And **out of the ground** the LORD God **formed** every beast of the field, and every fowl of the air,"*

Again, it's important to specify that God did **not** restore the animals he once destroyed. God gave the earth **permission** to form the animals He **called forth**; however, God **did not touch** the animals.

Now God 'creates' man:

Genesis 1:26–28, 31 KJV, *"²⁶And God said, **Let** us make man in our image, after our likeness: and let them have dominion over the fish of the sea, and over the fowl of the air, and over the cattle, **and over all the earth,** and over every creeping thing that creepeth upon the earth.²⁷ So God **created** man in his own image, in the image of God **created** he him, male and female **created** he them.* ²⁸ *And God blessed them, and God* *said to them, be fruitful and multiply and* **replenish** *the earth, and* **subdue** *it. And have dominion over the fish of the sea, and over the fowl of the air, and over every living thing that moveth upon the earth."* (now I skip to verse 31) *[31] And God saw every thing that he had made, and behold, it was very good. And the evening and the morning were the sixth day."*

Here on the sixth day, God **spoke** into existence the animals from the dust of the ground. However, God made or **formed** man, male and female, from the dust of the ground. God put his **hand** on man. The female was created **within** the male. Man became a 'living' being when God breathed His breath of life into man's nostrils. **Genesis 2:7 KJV,** *"And the LORD God formed man of the dust of the ground, and breathed into his nostrils the breath of life; and man became a living soul."*

The female was created **within** the male. **Genesis 2:21-22 KJV,** *"And the LORD God caused a deep sleep to fall upon Adam, and he slept: and he took one of his ribs, and closed up the flesh instead thereof, [22] and the rib, which the LORD God had taken from man,* **made** *he a woman, and brought her to the man."*

Adam was a proper name (see note at the end of 'conclusion'), which both of them were called. Adam did not name his wife Eve until after the fall.

The Hebrew word for **made** in verse [22] is '**panah**' which means to build. God '**built**' the woman from the part of her he took out of the man.

Now God rests from His work of '**restoration**' and '**creation**':

<u>Genesis 2:1-3 KJV,</u> *"[1] Thus the heavens and the earth were finished, and all the hosts of them. [2] And on the seventh day God ended his work which he had made, and he rested on the seventh day from all his work which he had made. [3] And God blessed the seventh day, and sanctified it: because he hath rested from all his work which God **created** and **made**."*

Chapter Conclusion:

I titled this chapter 'God's Restoration and Creation' to make the point of both occurring. I believe the contents of this chapter bring that point to light. Again, let's look at <u>**Jeremiah 4:27**</u> *"For thus the LORD said; The whole land will be desolate,* ***yet I will not make a full end.****"* In that verse, God is **revealing** His plan for the restoration of the earth He destroyed.

From using the Hebrew meanings of the words, **let, create,** and **make (or made)**, scripture reveals that God **restored** the **earth** from its destroyed state in

<u>**Genesis 1:2 KJV,**</u> *"And the earth was without form, and void; and darkness was upon the face of the deep! And the Spirit of God moved upon the face of the waters,"* back into its perfect state in <u>**Genesis 1:1 KJV,**</u> *"In the beginning God created the heaven(s) and the earth."*

We are also shown that God **created** animals and man. The animals God created were **new creatures** that He 'spoke' into existence. God 'formed' man from the dust of the ground **in the image of God. God touched the man.**

In summary, God 'restored' the earth from <u>**Genesis 1:3-19**</u> and 'creates' from <u>**Genesis 1:20-23.**</u>

<u>Why did God tell Adam to 'replenish and 'subdue' the earth?</u>

To understand God's revelation of the answer, first, let's look at the words **replenish** and **subdue.**

<u>Let's start with the definitions of **replenish** in English and Hebrew as follows:</u>

Replenish (English) - *verb* – fill something up **again, restore** to a former level or condition.

The Hebrew verb for **replenish** means fill. This is the same meaning as for the verb 'plenish,' which means to fill up, stock, furnish.

In this instance, we need to allow the Bible to interpret itself for the word **replenish.** For this, let's go to <u>**Genesis 9:1 KJV,**</u> *"And God blessed Noah and his sons, and said to them, Be fruitful and multiply and* ***replenish*** *the earth."*

In that account, we know that the inhabitants of the earth were destroyed by the flood, and God told Noah and his sons to **replenish** the earth. From this, we can see that the intent of the word **'replenish'** given to Adam (name of both male and female) was to 'fill something up **again, restore** to a former level or condition.'

<u>Now let's look at the word **subdue** in English and Hebrew.</u>

Subdue (English) – *verb* – to overcome, quieten, or bring under control.

Subdue (Hebrew definition given from Strongs Concordance) – *'kabash'* – meaning – brought into bondage.

The definitions of the word **subdue** reveal what God was commanding Adam (name of both male and female) when God said in **Genesis 1:28,** *"And God blessed them, and God said to them, be fruitful and multiply and* ***replenish*** *the earth, and* ***subdue*** *it."*

There was an 'enemy' present whom Adam (name of both male and female) were commanded to **subdue.** How were they to **subdue** the enemy? By an act of **obedience** on their part to God's command **not** to eat from 'The Tree of The Knowledge of Good and Evil".

Genesis 3:15-16, *"15And the LORD God took the man, and put him into the garden of Eden to dress it and to keep it. 16And the LORD God commanded the man, saying, Of every tree of the garden thou mayest freely eat: 17but of the tree of the knowledge of good and evil, thou shalt not eat of it: for in the day that thou eatest thereof thou shalt surely die."*

<u>Adam's name:</u>

Note: Both male and female were named 'Adam.' Adam was a 'proper' name given by God for 'human' or 'mankind.' Adam named his wife Eve **after the fall. <u>Genesis 3:20,</u>** *"And Adam **called his wife's name Eve**, because she was the mother of all living."*

There is **so much more** to be said about 'the fall of Adam', but it doesn't fit with the scope of this book. I encourage you to read and study it for yourself.

Chapter 7

God's Stern Rebuke

*"Then The Lord answered Job out of the whirlwind, and said, Who is this that darkenth counsel **by words without knowledge**?"* **Job 38:1-2**

As I stated in the introduction, this book is not about the Gospel message exclusively. Neither is it about the Christian doctrines on salvation which are indisputable.

Also, the revelatory facts presented in this book are not currently shared by all Christians, and we can respectfully agree to disagree.

However, God is issuing to some Christians a stern rebuke! We cannot continue to stick our heads in the sand and deny the facts that 'legitimate' science has discovered. Legitimate science proves the accuracy of the Bible, and it's not the other way around!

It is time for the Christians who are saying that 'legitimate' science is **evil** to be delivered from a **spirit of ignorance invited in by arrogance and pride.** It is time for us to **humble** ourselves in order to receive the full manifestation of God, to the point He has revealed Himself and His creation.

I repeat. I am **not** saying to embrace theories that set out to deny the existence of God. **Do not even entertain them!** What I **am** saying is that once we proclaim what God reveals in His word concerning the title of this book, then those illegitimate theories can be rightly opposed. Maybe even by some who now believe them!

We must never forget that it's not just about us! It's also about reaching the lost for God's Kingdom. Also, know this, you are **not** defending God by your denial of 'legitimate' scientific facts, brought on by pride, arrogance, and lack of knowledge. Rather you are subjecting God to ridicule and causing Him to appear small and finite! You are also blocking the path for many to be saved. **Repent!**